$10
Art

12/3

BIRKET FOSTER, R.W.S.

IN THE SAME SERIES

GEORGE MORLAND

·

JOHN PETTIE, R.A., H.R.S.A.

·

KATE GREENAWAY

A. AND C. BLACK . SOHO SQUARE . LONDON, W.

AGENTS

AMERICA . . . THE MACMILLAN COMPANY
64 & 66 FIFTH AVENUE, NEW YORK

AUSTRALASIA . OXFORD UNIVERSITY PRESS
205 FLINDERS LANE, MELBOURNE

CANADA . . . THE MACMILLAN COMPANY OF CANADA, LTD.
27 RICHMOND STREET WEST, TORONTO

INDIA . . . . MACMILLAN & COMPANY, LTD.
MACMILLAN BUILDING, BOMBAY
309 BOW BAZAAR STREET, CALCUTTA

BIRKET FOSTER

R.W.S.

SIXTEEN EXAMPLES IN COLOUR
OF THE ARTIST'S WORK

WITH
AN INTRODUCTION
BY
H. M. CUNDALL, I.S.O., F.S.A.

PUBLISHED BY A. & C. BLACK
4, 5 & 6 SOHO SQUARE, LONDON
MCMX

LIST OF PLATES

BIRKET FOSTER

THE dainty water-colour paintings executed by Birket Foster probably appeal to the majority of the British public more than the work of any other artist.

For many years during the early part of his career he was engaged in drawing on wood-blocks for the engraver, from which he acquired a minuteness in detail that continued to pervade his paintings in later life. The result was that he produced scenes from Nature with an exact-ness that the most uninitiated in art are able to understand and appreciate. The chief features, however, in Birket Foster's paintings are the poetic feeling with which he indued them, and the care and felicity with which his compositions were selected. These qualities lend a great charm to his drawings, and especially to those representing the homely scenes, so frequently selected from that picturesque part of Surrey, where he lived for many years. He revelled in sunny landscapes, with sheep roaming in the distance and with rustic children playing in the foreground ; he was also attracted by peaceful red-brick cottages covered with thatch, and enlivened by domestic scenes. It is perhaps by these rural paintings that the artist is best known. He, however, wandered far afield in search of the picturesque ; he was an indefatigable painter,

and produced works selected from all parts of
England, Wales, and Scotland. Birket Foster
was especially partial to the Northern counties
and the district surrounding his native town in
Northumberland. His rambles were not con-
fined solely to his own country; he travelled
frequently on the Continent; Venice, as well as
the Rhine, had its charms for him. The picturesque scenery of Brittany has also been portrayed
by his brush, and on one occasion he went as far
as Spain and Morocco in pursuit of his art.

Birket Foster, as he is generally known, or
Myles Birket Foster, to give him his full name,
was born at North Shields on February 4, 1825.
His ancestors held good social positions for
many generations in the North Country, and
were staunch members of the Society of Friends.
One, Sarah Forster, as the family name was
originally spelt, married a descendant of Mar-
garet Fell of Swathmoor Hall, who, after the
death of her first husband, Judge Fell, was united
to George Fox, the founder of the Quakers.

In 1830 the artist's father migrated with his
family to London, voyaging all the way by sea.
He took up his residence at 40 Charlotte Street,
Portland Place, and founded the well-known
firm of M. B. Foster and Sons.

Quitting school at an early age, young Birket
Foster was at first placed in his father's business;

but, owing to an accident, he did not remain long in that position.

As the youth showed a decided tendency towards art, his father consulted a Mr. Stone, a die-engraver, with whom he had a slight acquaintance, and it was arranged that the son should be apprenticed to him. Before, however, the articles of apprenticeship could be signed, Mr. Stone unfortunately committed suicide. In his dilemma the father next sought the assistance of a fellow-townsman, Ebenezer Landells, who at that time had established his reputation as a wood-engraver. He offered to take the boy into his business to see whether the work would suit him. The offer was accepted, and the day on which Birket Foster entered Landells' office may be said to be the commencement of his artistic career.

In 1841 Landells, in conjunction with Henry Mayhew, Mark Lemon, and others, started *Punch*. Most of the early woodcuts for this publication were produced in Landells' office ; Birket Foster was employed to draw and cut numerous initial letters, and on one occasion he was entrusted to make a full-page political cartoon representing Lord John Russell as Jack Sheppard.

When *The Illustrated London News* was commenced by Herbert Ingram in 1842, Landells was engaged to produce many of the illustrations, and Birket Foster was employed by him in making drawings for them. This he continued to do for many years after he left Landells' establishment. The most characteristic works of Birket Foster for this periodical were the charming engravings which appeared in the musical supplements and the Christmas numbers. He also made many drawings for *The Illustrated London Almanack* for 1848 and subsequent years.

At this period our artist was greatly sought after by publishers to execute pencil drawings for wood-engravings for books, and from the year 1847 to 1863 more than eighty different volumes, produced by various firms, were illustrated by dainty engravings after his drawings.

After the year 1858 Birket Foster practically abandoned the drawing on wood-blocks, and devoted himself almost entirely to water-colour painting. He received little or no instruction in the art, and in later years, when he was frequently pestered by persons asking him to give them lessons in painting, he used to say that he never received any lessons, so he never gave them, believing the best instruction to be obtained from studying the great masters. He was a profound admirer of Turner and Clarkson Stanfield, and it is probable that he was more influenced by the latter's works than by those of any other artist, especially with regard to composition. He delighted to surround himself with paintings by these and other artists.

With regard to his method of working, Birket Foster's early training for drawing on wood-blocks considerably influenced his water-colour work, which was very dissimilar to the "wash" methods of the early school of water-colour painters. He, indeed, worked with his brush as dry as it well could be, and probably no artist in using the medium of water-colours ever used so little water. Of course, all painting may be said to be drawing with a brush, but Birket Foster's was practically drawing to a peculiar degree, not washing with a brush. He used a very fine brush with very little paint in it, and owing to his habit of frequently putting it between his lips to make the point of it as fine as possible, it used to be said that the paint came out of the artist's head.

Birket Foster worked very rapidly in his own way of obtaining the effects he desired, and his remarkable gift for composition enabled him to people his scenes with wonderful facility and felicity. He never engaged a professional model; his children were all sketched from the rustic boys and girls, whom he found in the course of his wanderings.

In 1860 Birket Foster was unanimously elected an associate of the Old Water-Colour Society, and became a full member two years afterwards.

He greatly appreciated the honour conferred upon him, and thoroughly gave his best interests to the Society.

He was a most prolific worker, and beside the large number of water-colour paintings exhibited at the Old Society, to which he contributed more than four hundred and fifty, many of his drawings were bought by the picture-dealers straight from his studio, and in some cases he received direct commissions for paintings from collectors.

Birket Foster, like many other water-colour artists, turned his attention to painting in oils, and for the nine years, 1869 to 1877, he regularly contributed oil paintings, thirteen in all, to the Exhibitions at the Royal Academy, but after that period he abandoned this medium, as he found that his little water-colour gems were far more appreciated by the public. In 1876 Foster was elected a member of the Royal Academy of Berlin.

Although the rural scenery of his native country had its peculiar charms for his pencil, still Birket Foster was greatly attracted by the grander views to be obtained on the Continent. His early visits were made to the Rhine, but subsequently the Italian lakes and Venice were his favourite hunting grounds in search for "bits" to sketch. The word "bits" is particularly applicable in the case of Birket Foster, for he almost invariably preferred to make a drawing of some detail rather than a broad landscape. He used to say that the mountain scenery of Switzerland was too panoramic and had no attractions for him. It is somewhat remarkable that whilst he relied to a great extent on lanes and fields, and hedgerows and rustic children, for his English drawings, the views for his Continental paintings were largely selected from towns with architectural details introduced into them.

The first visit made to the Continent by Birket Foster was in 1852, when he was commissioned by a publisher, who was bringing out an illustrated edition of "Hyperion," by Longfellow, to follow in the footsteps of Paul Flemming, and to depict on the spot the varied scenes amid which the poet had laid the incidents of his story. Paul Flemming, as is well known, was Longfellow himself, and the romance was a passage in the author's own life.

From that date Foster made almost annual tours along the Rhine and through Switzerland, but it was not until the year 1868 that he was first able to feast his eyes upon the beauties of Venice, and afterwards he made numerous subsequent trips to Italy.

Our artist for many years resided at St. John's Wood, and when he took seriously to water-colour painting he at first selected his subjects from the fields about Hampstead and Highgate. He soon, however, wandered farther afield, and was attracted by the picturesque scenery of Surrey. During his wanderings in this delightful county he found himself at Witley, near Godalming, and he resolved to have a residence there.

It cannot be said that Witley was "discovered" by Birket Foster, for other artists were there before him. J. C. Hook, R.A., had already built himself a residence and studio upon an eminence with a beautiful view overlooking the Weald of Surrey. There can, however, be no doubt that the genial disposition and the liberal hospitality of the owner of "The Hill" afterwards attracted many of his fellow-artists to the neighbourhood.

Witley station stands at a spot where the railway emerges from a deep cutting with pine woods on either side, and at this period there were but few houses or even cottages in the vicinity, for the village itself lies a mile and a quarter to the northward; but Birket Foster managed to secure the possession of a picturesque cottage called "Tigbourne," situated by the corner of the road leading to Hambledon at the foot of Wormley Hill, and resided there during the summer months.

Birket Foster eventually became so pleased with the neighbourhood that he determined to take up his permanent abode at Witley. After lengthy negotiations, he secured a beautiful site, between Wormley Hill and the railway station, on which he erected a house which was called "The Hill," and finally quitted St. John's Wood. He was practically his own architect, and residing near by at his cottage, he was enabled personally to superintend the erection of the entire building. In order that its newness should not offend the artistic eye, he purchased as many weather-worn tiles off the old cottages in the neighbourhood as possible, and placed them on the roof of his house. A great amount of care was bestowed on the internal decorations. William Morris was consulted, and Burne-Jones painted seven canvases illustrating the legend of St. George and the Dragon, which formed a frieze round three sides of the dining-room. Burne-Jones was also commissioned to make many other designs for the adornment of "The Hill"; the decorated tiles round the fire-places and stained glass in the windows were all designed by him. He also painted a large screen of eight folds, upon which were sixteen events of the life of St. Frideswide. These scenes were afterwards reproduced in the windows of Christ Church Cathedral at Oxford.

"The Hill" was an open house to all Birket

Foster's friends, and particularly to his brother-artists. He was never more pleased than when he was entertaining his guests, and being specially fond of music, many of the social gatherings were enhanced by musical performances.

One of the most frequent visitors was Frederick Walker, A.R.A. : he was a special favourite, at all times welcome, and was one of the few who had an influence on Birket Foster's painting, especially his figures. He was in the habit of going to Witley whenever he felt inclined, without waiting for an invitation, a bedroom known as "Freddy's room" being reserved for him. Walker had an immense love for the place, which he called "Paradise," and greatly regretted that he had not sufficient money to purchase a cottage which J. C. Hook, R.A., had built near his house, the situation of which Walker considered "romantic—such a sweep of glorious country."

Another constant visitor was Charles Keene, the celebrated black and white artist of *Punch*. After Birket Foster had removed from "Tigbourne Cottage" he still rented it that he might make sure of the presence of an agreeable and congenial occupant, and persuaded Keene to become a tenant. Keene was greatly delighted with this retreat, of which he wrote :—

"The stillness here after London is delicious. The only sound is the ring of the village blacksmith's hammer in the distance or the occasional cluck of a hen, and the wind roars through the trees of a night, which lulls me pleasantly to sleep."

As may be seen by glancing through the titles of his exhibited paintings, the neighbourhood around Witley had a great charm for Birket Foster, and drawings made on Hambledon Common and in the village of Chiddingfold—with their picturesque cottages roofed with thatch or red tiles, now fast disappearing, and their leafy lanes with happy children gathering wild-flowers, or the beautiful view from his own residence overlooking the Surrey Weald, with Hindhead and Blackdown in the distance and glimpses of the Brighton Downs beyond—are most appreciated by the public, and it is by these paintings he is best known.

Birket Foster, as already stated, made very many tours through different parts of England and Scotland, and although he was not what may be termed a seascape artist, he was fond of making drawings of children playing on the sea-shore. Later in life he revisited many of the watering-places which he depicted for *The Illustrated London News* in his early days, and instead of sketches for wood-blocks, he painted many charming little scenes.

Another phase of Birket Foster's art was his

love for painting fruit and flowers. He was greatly attracted by William Hunt's work. As may be expected, the same stippling in paintings by Hunt appears in works of Foster; but whilst the former nearly always painted his fruit pieces the same size as in Nature, the latter produced almost miniature representations of them.

In 1893 Birket Foster was attacked by a serious illness, and yielding to the pressure of medical advice, he was obliged to abandon much of his work and reluctantly to give up " The Hill." He removed to " Braeside," Weybridge, and here he resided quietly, devoting himself to his painting as much as possible, until his death, which occurred six years later. He was buried in Witley churchyard; a Celtic cross, with the simple inscription, "In memory of Birket Foster. Born Feb. 4th, 1825. Died March 27th, 1899," marks the spot where lie the remains of this great water-colour artist, who painted English landscape with such a pure feeling and high perception of the beauty of Nature.

Birket Foster was twice married—firstly, in 1850, to his cousin, Ann Spence, by whom he had five children, three sons and two daughters ; and secondly, in 1864, to Frances Watson, a sister to John Dawson Watson, the well-known painter and member of the Old Water-Colour Society.